AMAZ ECHO Show 8 2nd Gen 2021 USER MANUAL

The Complete Beginners And Senior User Guide On How To Setup And Use The Latest 2nd Generation Echo Show 8 With Updated Alexa Tips And Tricks

Thomas Mallack

Table of Contents

CHAPTER ONE

Introducing Amazon Echo Show 8 (2nd generation)

Amazon Echo Show 8 has not been around for a long time, but during this period it really took on the role of the middle child of the Echo Show line. Offering more features and functionality than the Amazon Echo Show 5 at a much lower price than the Amazon Echo Show 10, the Amazon Echo Show offers a lot of value for the price tag.

The 2nd generation of the mid-range smart display offers a new 13-megapixel wide-angle camera that can digitally record and scale video calls and a new super octa-core processor that makes the display even better. switch between programs. There are also dual stereo speakers and an 8-inch HD display with adaptive colors. At the moment, the result looks like a functional and aesthetically pleasing smart display that can call family and friends and play your favorite songs and shows from your favorite shows. Services such as Amazon Music Unlimited and Amazon Prime Video. If you're new to smart home space and looking for a smart display, the all-new Amazon Echo Show 8 may be a good choice for you.

Design

Admittedly, there is no huge aesthetic difference between the old Amazon Echo Show 8 and the new Amazon Echo Show 8 - the cases are almost the same. At the front, you will find a new 13-megapixel camera and an 8-inch 1280 x 800 display, but there is nothing else to see. At the top of the Echo Show 8, there is volume up / down controls and Alexa, but there is also a mute button to mute the microphone and a slide to close the camera. It is not negotiable for privacy lovers, and it's great to have it here.

Speaking of microphones, the Echo Show 8 (2021) also has the same four-microphone configuration as its mid-range and wide-range predecessor, which can hear you to loud music - however, sometimes you may need to repeat statements before Alexa can hear you.

The 2021 Echo Show 8 possesses an octa-core MediaTek MT8183, when compared to the previous Echo Show 8, which operates with MediaTek MT 8163.

Theoretically, this should make the smart display a little faster than the current Echo Show 8 predecessor. In practice, however, it's hard for us to prove it - in fact, they're both relatively clever, although the video seems to start a little faster in the new Echo Show. Last but not least are the dual 2-inch speakers hidden behind the mesh back of the Amazon Echo Show 8. These speakers are not the last of all the speakers (see below), but having two drivers is better than one.

New camera

As already mentioned, the 13-megapixel camera with a higher resolution is the only significant change on the Echo Show 8 compared to the previous 1-megapixel model. This is definitely clearer for video calls and home surveillance, thanks to the wide-angle view, which can automatically move and scale the face during a conversation. However, despite the large changes in megapixels, it is not noticeably sharper; even with 13 megapixels, the small lens and the fact that the Echo Show can be used indoors mean that noise and softness are easily noticeable.

During testing, I was unable to make small parts on the adjacent wall, even when squeezing to enlarge. However, the ability to do this and not allow photos to turn into a bunch of pixels is a noticeable improvement over the previous model. Colors tend to look accurate, and images look bright and easily visible in most interior lighting. And while the Echo Show 8 doesn't physically appeal to you like the Echo Show 10, it can automatically pan and zoom your face, making video chats easier and more accessible than the previous model.

Performance

So what does Amazon Echo Show 8 like to use? Well, it's pretty much like many other Amazon Echo Show devices. It's an intuitive display - albeit a little lower than we'd like - with a ton of information about your day. The Show will usually contain a notification on the screen about what Alexa can do ("Alexa, call") or about events in your calendar or facts and weather information for your area.

Of course, making calls are all about the new Amazon Echo Show 8, so you'll find its greatest power there. With a 13-megapixel camera, call quality will be greatly improved for you with very little grain, even in poor lighting conditions. The 13-megapixel camera makes images look clearer in most cases, but also allows Amazon Echo Show 8 to zoom in when you're sitting away from the camera - it does the little trick if you can't always sit too close to your show.

How useful you get this feature depends on how many video calls you to make (Echo currently supports Echo-to-Echo and Zoom calls), but we appreciate it. Amazon has dedicated this feature at a time when we spend more time than ever on video calls. However, we can't talk about Amazon's smart device, let alone Alexa. Determining what Alexa can do is based on whether you already have an Alexa device, or by reviewing some basic tutorials. However, Alexa's functionality has evolved significantly over the years thanks to an ever-growing skills library that can do more than you could imagine, or learn from textbooks. For example, Alexa can tell you how good the air quality is around you when you ask, "Alexa, how is the air quality today?" or can tell you how to pronounce words in another language (however, it can't translate real-time conversations like Google).

However, for every question that Alexa can answer, there are more than half a dozen others that she can't answer - which can be frustrating for people who have trouble understanding when asked a question. It becomes too difficult for Alexa to answer ("Alexa, what's the risk?" Vs. "Alexa, who's the first to take the risk?") And often requires you to memorize Alexa's commands verbatim.

In terms of sound quality, Amazon Echo Show 8 has undoubtedly improved the midrange to make dialogues and conversations much clearer, but this is due to the high and low levels of the sound spectrum.

Is there a silver lining here? It's easy to group Alexa speakers together so they can all play the same song in different rooms. This is ideal if you put Amazon Echo Show 8 in the kitchen and there is something more important in your living room, such as Amazon Echo Studio, which plays the same song. The sound quality of the Amazon Echo Show 8 itself can still be expected, but when it is part of a larger group, it stands out little among the crowd.

It's also a similar story to display. The Amazon Echo Show 8 1280 x 800 display won't let you down - especially compared to a tablet or laptop - but you'll still be able to watch cooking videos or a short show on Amazon Prime Video. Of course, the picture is not cinematic, especially without HDR support, but it is quite decent for its size.

CHAPTER TWO

How to Set Up Echo Show 8

Before proceeding with the setup, make sure you have Wi-Fi credentials and Amazon accounts. First, choose the place where you want your Echo Show to be, and plug it in. It will start immediately.

Connect to Wi-Fi

- Select your Wi-Fi network from the list.
- Use the virtual keyboard to enter your Wi-Fi password.

- enter the WiFi password
- When finished, click Finish.

Connect your Amazon account

- Input the mobile number or email address and passcode your Amazon account is connected with.

Sign in with your Amazon account

Email Address or Phone Number

Password

To create a new account, visit Amazon.com   SIGN IN

- Click Sign in when you're done.

If you have set up two-factor authentication, you will be prompted to do so on the next screen after clicking Login.

- Enter the code from the authentication program and tap Sign in.

amazon

Two-Step Verification

Enter the code generated by your Authenticator App

Enter code

☐ Don't ask for codes on this device

Sign In

- Didn't receive the code?

Conditions of Use   Privacy Notice   Help

© 1996-2017, Amazon.com, Inc. or its affiliates

Confirm the time zone / TC

North America ▼

Eastern Daylight Time
New York, United States ▼

CONTINUE

- enter the time zone

- Click Continue.

- Carefully read the terms of your new Amazon Echo Show.

- When you are sure you understand, click Continue.

Update your device

Amazon is always adding new features and capabilities to your Amazon Echo Show.

- Click Install Now to download and install these updates.

Device updates ready

Your Echo device will be updated to the latest software. This could take about 10 minutes.

INSTALL NOW

- After the update is complete, the device will reboot itself.

Your new Amazon Echo Show will show a short introductory video about its features and commands that you can use.

Reset Echo Show

If your Echo does not respond or you want to delete the device settings, reset the device to the factory settings. These steps also work with Echo Spot.

Advice. Problems with Echo? First, reboot the device to see if it solves the problem. Just unplug the power adapter from the device or outlet and plug it in again.

- Press and hold the mute and volume down buttons until you see the Amazon logo (approximately 15 seconds).
- When prompted, follow the on-screen instructions to set up your device.

CHAPTER THREE

How to use Alexa as a home intercom

If you have two or more smart Amazon Echo speakers, you can use the Drop-In feature to act as an intercom or broadcast recorded messages to each Alexa speaker in your home. Launching allows you to listen through the microphone of another Alexa device - convenient if you want to register in your child's bedroom. Just say "Alexa, visit [room name]" and assuming you named the Echo speakers after the rooms they are in, it should work fine.

Similarly, Alexa can also be used for household ads. Instead of getting on a specific Alexa device, it transmits the recorded message through any compatible device. These include all Echo speakers and displays, as well as Sonos speakers and even smart thermostats equipped with Ecobee.

To broadcast a message to anyone who speaks on Alexa at the same time, say, "Alexa is broadcasting [your message]." This is useful for letting your family know that you are leaving or that dinner is ready.

Print shopping lists, worksheets, crossword

With the new free update, you can now ask your Alexa voice assistant to print crossword puzzles and sudoku puzzles on demand. The assistant can also print your shopping and to-do lists from the Alexa app, or print out recipes, graph paper, backing, mazes to solve, coloring pictures, and student worksheets. Amazon insisted that the new feature works with dozens of wireless printers from Brother, HP, Epson, and Canon. You can find a full list of compatible printers here, or just say "Alexa, find my printer" to see if your printer works with an assistant.

Or open the Alexa smartphone app, then tap Devices at the bottom right, then the + icon in the upper right corner, and then tap Add Device. The feature, called Alexa Print, works with all second-generation and newer Echo smartphones and displays. Once you have detected and configured Alexa, all you have to do is ask your assistant to print something. These can be shopping lists and to-do lists that you have created in Alexa, or by talking to an assistant, or even recipes created by AllRecipes. Just ask for a food offer and it will be printed.

We believe that the best printouts here are daily crossword puzzles, mazes, and sudoku puzzles. What's especially good at first is how you can one day ask for a crossword puzzle and then ask Alexa to print out the answer the next day (or immediately if you're stuck). You can also invite crossword puzzles and answers for the last seven days. Just say, "Alexa, print me a crossword puzzle last Sunday."

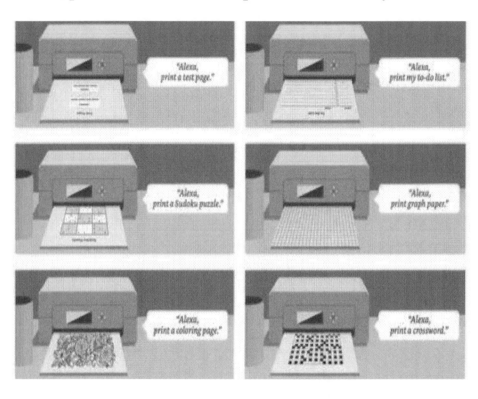

Amazon is working with JumpStart Academy to create worksheets for children printed by Alexa. You can invite worksheets on specific subjects or topics, such as multiplication or the solar system, and indicate which class is right for your child. For example, you can say, "Alexa, print a layer on one extra sheet" or, "Alexa, print a fourth-class solar system letter."

Finally, Alexa can print out some paperwork with the rules. You can ask for a test page, a checker, or plain backing paper to write a letter. Another bonus is connecting Alexa to the printer so that the assistant notifies you when the ink is low and offers to order more. With the `` smart rearrangement " system, Alexa can also be set to automatically order extra ink or toner when the printer runs out.

Activate Alexa automatic Hunches

Voice assistants can now automatically control your smart home on your behalf. Amazon Voice Assistant from Amazon can guess your intentions for several years since the launch of a feature called `` haunches " in 2018. However, although Alexa may decide that you may need to, for example, turn off the lights or lower the thermostat based on your familiar activity, the assistant will ask permission before acting.

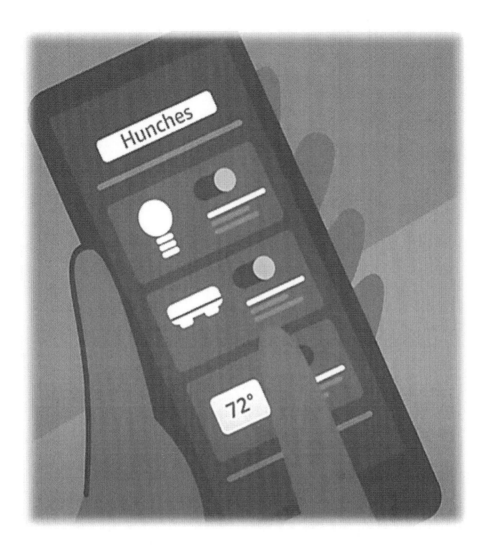

Today, however, Amazon is quite confident in Alexa's capabilities that the voice assistant can be configured to automatically act on these guesses without first asking permission. Hunches are created by Alexa's artificial intelligence and are based on how you regularly interact with an assistant to manage your smart home. If you turn off the same smart lights every night at the same time before going to bed, Alexa will do so silently.

With a premonition on, Alex will ask if you want the light to turn off at this particular time. But with the new automated system turned on, the assistant will switch the switch for you without asking permission. Following this example, Alex also knows if you want to leave a certain light on all night, such as the light at the front door, and will eventually do so without asking.

You can use the Alexa application to authorize an assistant to act on certain assumptions on your behalf. Other examples include how Alexa can activate your robotic vacuum cleaner when you're outdoors or when you're usually asked to turn it on. Similarly, Alexa can control your smart thermostat by making the same settings on your behalf as usual.

"Instead of reducing the heat or running a robot vacuum before going to work, just go out the door and Alexa will be able to take care of everything else," says Amazon, adding that the system works "whether smart A light bulb or a fully connected house ". Earlier, if Alex sensed something, it would send a message from your Echo speaker saying, "I think you left the kitchen light on, do you want me to turn it off?"

Enable Alexa Hunches

Follow these instructions to get started with the new Alexa automatic hunches:

- Open Alexa on your smartphone
- Tap the "More" icon in the lower right corner, then "Settings"
- Scroll down and tap Hunches
- Choose "set up automatic hunches"

From there, you can choose which hunches you want Alexa to act on automatically and what you want the assistant to ask first. Today, the warning system is only available in the United States, with the possibility of wider implementation later.

How to track the energy consumption of your smart home with Alexa

The new Alexa power console is compatible with a wide range of headlights and smart plugs. A new feature called Alexa Power Dashboard brought US users to the US and tracks power consumption with a wide range of smart home devices connected to a Wi-Fi network. Fi and your Alexa system. Although still unpopular today, the Energy dashboard works with several smart lights, thermostats, and smart plugs - the latter being the most useful as it allows Alexa to track the energy usage of anything plugged into the plug.

This may include a TV or in these cold winter months, such as an electric heater. In summer, you can use this feature to control how much energy your desk fan or office air conditioner consumes. The Alexa Energy dashboard also includes an equally new auto-anticipation feature, where Alexa controls smart devices in your home based on your usage habits. With two systems working together, Alexa can turn off your smart lights when you go to bed at night, helping to reduce your energy bills.

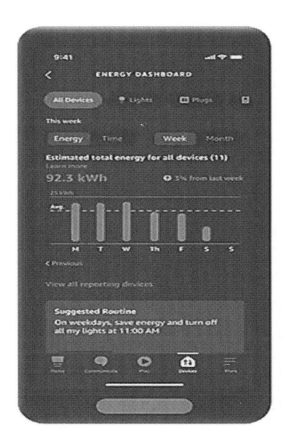

Amazon says, "If Alexa guesses you forgot to turn off the lights and no one is home or everyone goes to bed, Alexa can automatically turn it off for you."

How to turn Echo Show into a digital photo frame
The device scrolls through your holiday photos and photos of children once. Well, many of us now have an advanced digital photo frame in our living rooms, kitchens, and bedrooms in the form of the Amazon Echo Show. So how

do you turn an Echo Show into a digital photo frame that displays your photos by scrolling information on its screen?

Upload photos to Amazon Photos

To date, the easiest way to get around this is to use another Amazon service - Amazon Photos. If you own an Echo Show, you almost certainly already have Amazon Prime, and that gives you plenty of free storage space in Amazon Photos. Sign in with your Amazon credentials and upload as many photos as you want to show on your Echo Show.

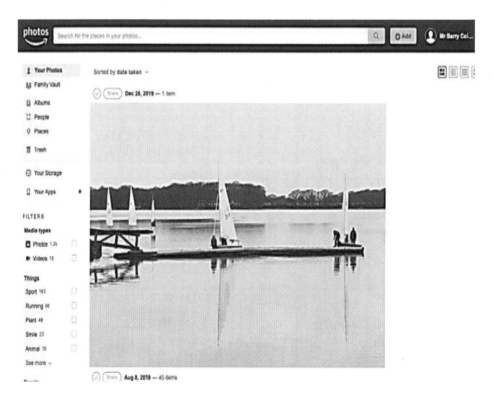

Put all your photos in one album

In the next step, you will be prompted to select the photo album you want to use for the echo show for the wallpaper/dial. It makes sense to create a folder in Amazon Photos specifically for this purpose so that random photos do not appear on your device. On the Amazon Photos page, click Albums, and then click Create Album. Give it a name like "Show Background" and then add as many photos as you want to use. Landscape photos work much better because they match the aspect ratio of the screen.

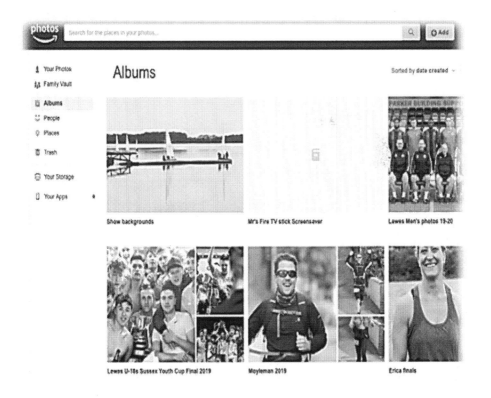

Immerse yourself in the Echo Show settings

Go to your Echo Show and say "Alexa, go to settings". On the screen that appears, select Home screen and Clock, then Clock, then Personal image. Select Amazon Photos on the next screen and you will be presented with a list of albums in your account. Select the album "Show your wallpaper" and you can show it as wallpaper or dial.

Different ways

You can do this with a photo taken on the phone as a new wallpaper. Open Alexa on your phone. Click "Devices" at the bottom right, then "Echo & Alexa" and select "Your Show" from the list. Now click on the Background screen of the home screen and scroll down to the Single Photo section, where you will find a button to upload the photo. I must say, this led to an error in my tests, but your mileage may be different.

How to remove Alexa recordings

The recording can be deleted by accessing the Alexa smartphone app for iPhone or Android. Just follow these instructions:

- Open Alexa App
- Click the 3-line icon in the top left corner
- Click Install
- Tap the Alexa account
- Click History

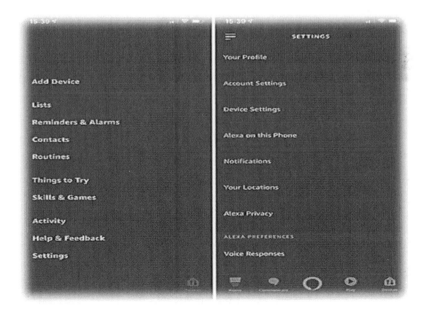

From here you can see and hear all the cases when Alexa recorded how you talked to her. Tap the recording, and then click Delete Audio to delete it from Amazon apps and servers.

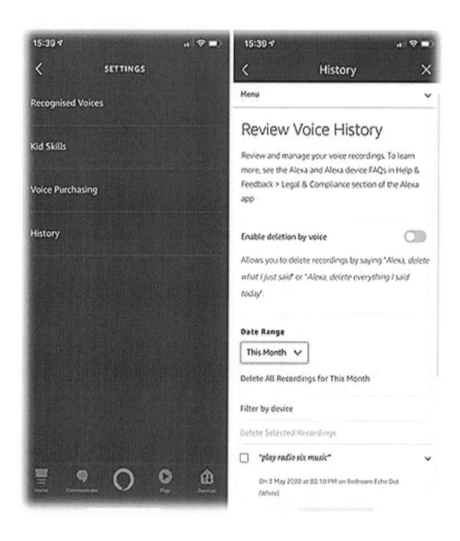

How to change Alexa name

You may want to change the word that Alexa answers, perhaps because you have a family member with the same name. To do this, open Alexa, and then follow these steps:

- Tap the three horizontal rows icon in the upper left corner
- Tap Settings -> Device Settings
- Navigate to the Alexa device you want to rename
- Now click Wake Word and then choose one of the options:
- Alexa (default)
- Echoes
- Computer
- Amazon
- How to teach Alex your voice

After giving permission, Alexa can find out your voice. As a result, the assistant will call you by name and be able to quickly order from your Amazon account whenever you ask. Alexa will also know who to call or send a text message to when asked, as it will have access to the right person's contacts, and content such as music and short news feeds can be adapted so that each user receives personalized messages.

First, open Alexa, tap the icon in the upper left corner and then select Settings -> Alexa Accounts -> Recognized Voices -> Your Voice.

Change Alexa accent

Although each option is female (unlike Google Assistant and Apple Siri), you can change both Alexa's voice accent and language. To do this, follow these instructions:

- Open Alexa
- Click the menu icon in the top left corner
- Tap Settings and then Device Settings
- Find the device whose voice you want to change and tap it
- Tap Language, then make a selection

How to make Alexa bilingual

Alexa has been bilingual since 2019, but initially, the assistant could only speak English and Spanish and was only available to American users. To date, however, Amazon has improved somewhat. Now, Alexa can speak English with any of the following people:

- German
- French
- French Canadians
- Japanese
- Spanish
- American-Spanish
- Hindi

To set it up, just say, "Alexa, speak English and French" or any other language you want to use from the list above. Alexa's new language features combine with existing English and Spanish pairs in the United States, English and Hindi in India, and Canadian English and French in Canada.

If you don't want Alexa to speak a second language anymore, just say, "Alexa, stop speaking French" or some other language you chose earlier.

Listen to music, radio, podcasts, and audiobooks with Alexa

This is a real cornerstone of the Alexa experience, and it's easy to set up - if you have an account with Amazon Music (which comes with Prime), Spotify, Apple Music, or

Deezer. You can also get free radio stations from TuneIn by simply saying, "Alexa, play [radio station name]". To add a music service (other than TuneIn) to your Alexa account, open Alexa, tap the icon in the upper left corner, and then select Settings -> Music -> Link new service.

CHAPTER FOUR

How to sync calendar with Alexa

Open Alexa and go to Settings -> Calendars to log in to the calendar service you are using and sync it with Alexa. Gmail, G Suite, Outlook, Office 365, and Apple iCloud are supported. Once logged in, you can ask Alexa about your day, add appointments to your calendar, or make changes to existing ones. Remember that anyone in the room can ask Alexa about these appointments, so if your Echo is in the common room, you may not want to turn this feature on.

Control reminders, alarms and timers with Alexa

You can add a reminder in Alexa or say, "Alexa, remind me to take out the trash at 7 pm on Wednesday," and the smartphone app will notify you at the right time. Set the alarms so that they work; just say, "Alexa, set the alarm at 7 am every day of the week" or set the alarm manually in the app. You can set a timer by saying, "Alexa, set a timer for x minutes," or you can call a timer and set several different timers at once - this can be especially useful when cooking. Any timer can be checked or canceled at any time; just ask how much time is left, or ask Alexa to cancel it.

How to make Alexa a translator

Asking Alexa to translate is as simple as saying, "Alexa, what is [a phrase] in [language]," and she will say it to you. In addition, you can enable the Translated skill, which translates English into 36 languages and has the added benefit of speaking more slowly or repeating yourself when you ask.

How to communicate with Alexa by typing instead of talking

There is a way to communicate with Alexa by typing in a smartphone app instead of speaking out loud. All you have to do is tap the text entry bar at the top of the screen where `` Assorted Alexa " is written, and enter your command. You can ask about the weather, ask Alexa to tell a joke, or control smart devices in your home without talking.

Group video call

This feature works with audio calls on all smart displays or Amazon Echo speakers, and can also be used to create video chats between users of the smart Echo Show display with a built-in camera. As soon as you set up, all you need to do is make a statement like, Alexa, call my family, and the call will be made. You first need to create a contact group in Alexa and then give the group a name. If you call the group `` my family '', it's just a case of asking Alexa to call the group to invite everyone to a video or audio chat.

Setting up a group call via Alexa

Take these instructions:

- Click the Alexa smartphone application for Android or iOS
- Click the "Communicate" button in the lower-left corner

- Now tap the person icon in the upper right corner
- Click Add New and then Add Group
- Click the Enable button to enable the new group call feature

A list of Alexa contacts will display. Check all the people you want to add to the group. You can add up to six, and you are the seventh member of the group. Now tap "Continue" at the bottom of the screen, give your group a name (things like "my family", "my friends" or "my colleagues" work best. Make sure it's a group name that's easy to pronounce and listen to the name that Alexa will use to set up a group call, everyone in the group will see his name, so be sure to name it correctly.

Once you've created a group, it will be listed at the top of your Alexa's contact list, ready to call. To make a call, just say, "Alexa, call [team name]." You can call a group from your smart speaker or Echo display, or from Alexa itself.

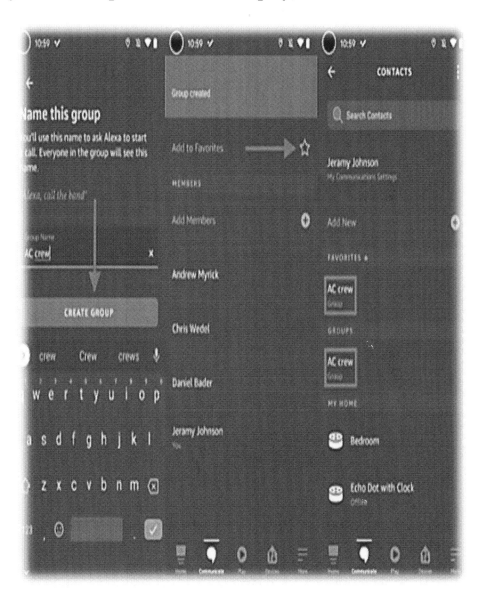

Group calls to Alexa are available in the following countries:

- Austria
- Australia
- Brazil
- Canada
- France
- Germany
- India
- Ireland
- Italy
- Mexico
- New Zealand
- Spain
- USA
- Great Britain

How to set up phone calls and text messages

Before you can make video or audio calls on your Echo Show, you need to set up this feature in Alexa itself.

- Open Alexa on your smartphone.

- Click the "Communicate" button on the bottom menu bar (it's like a chat bubble).
- Tap the people icon in the upper right corner of the screen.

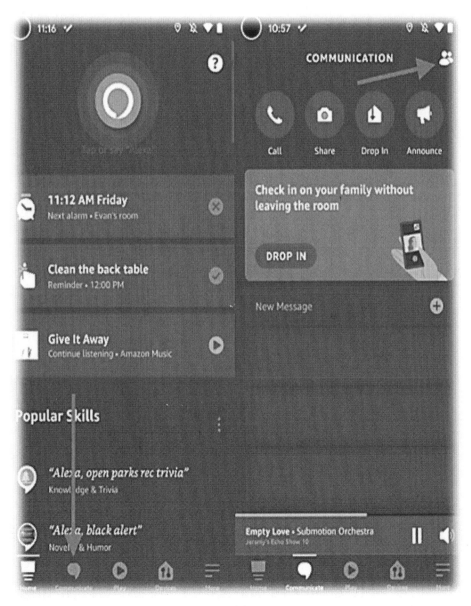

- Tap My connection settings.

- Tap your mobile to enter and confirm your phone number.

- Give Amazon permission to use phone and text messaging capabilities.

- Enter your phone's contact list when prompted for Alexa to call the person you requested.

Now you can start communicating with your contacts using Alexa or the smart column Echo or Echo Show. Calls are not just for smart speakers. It should also be noted that once you have enabled these communication features in Alexa and imported your contacts, you can make free voice calls to any mobile or landline phone to anyone between the US, Mexico, and Canada. So even if Grandma doesn't have an Echo or a smartphone, you can still ask Alex to call her if your hands are full while washing dishes or doing laundry urgently.

The only important thing is that you can't use Alexa or the Echo device to call emergency services (ie 911). However, there are some caveats. In the Amazon support forums, some users say that if you add 911 to your phone's contacts, Alexa will be able to dial this number on your request. In addition, with the new Amazon Guard Plus service from Amazon, Alexa can contact the emergency services on your behalf. Now that you've set up your communication settings in Alexa, make your first video call.

How to Make Video Calls

- From your Echo Show, ask Alexa to call one of your contacts.

- The person you are calling will see your picture/card with the ability to accept or reject the call by pressing their Echo Show home screen buttons or saying "Alexa Answer" or "Alexa ignore".
- When the call starts, say "play video" or tap the camcorder icon on the screen.
- If at any time you just want to turn off the video, you can say "turn off the video" or touch the camcorder icon again.
- If you want to hang up, say, Alexa, hang up.

It's easy, isn't it? Any of your contacts who have an Amazon Echo device with the communication option turned on will be able to hear your voice during calls. If they use the Echo Show or Alexa app on their smartphone, they can take a video call with you if they want. Another little trick you can do with the best Alexa speaker is to use an Alexa-specific feature called Drop In. Drop In can be used in your own home between a few echoes as a kind of intercom, where you can say, "Alex, come to Amy's room," so you can tell Amy that she still needs to cook.

Also, if your friends or family have turned on the Drop-In feature on their Echo device and decide to take incoming calls from you, you can ask Alexa to "visit Mom" so you can sign up and make sure your mom is okay.

How to Make Skype Calls

If you already have a Skype account, you can enable Skype calls from your Echo device by following these steps.

- Open Alexa on your smartphone.
- Tap the More menu tab at the bottom right of the screen.
- In the menu, open Settings.
- Click the Communication tab.
- In the Accounts section, tap Skype.
- Log in to your Skype account.
- Follow the on-screen prompts to connect your Skype account to your Alexa account.
- After connecting, you can ask Alexa to "call Grandpa on Skype" or say "Alexa, Skype Jason".

Echo Show Security Camera

Recently, there has been a new setting for some Amazon Echo Show smart displays that make them work more like a traditional security camera. Here's how to use it.

Start with the device you want as a security camera

To turn on the Echo Show device as a security camera, you need to go to its settings, not to the device settings in the Alexa application, keep in mind (although you end up using the program). Here). The first thing is to access your physical device, the smart Echo Show itself, scroll down from the upper part of the screen to access the main menu, and click Settings. (You can also say, "Alexa, go to settings.") From there, follow these steps:

1. To the right of Home Monitor, tap the switch to turn on the function.

2. A screen will appear with the message "Echo Show can help you keep track of your home ..." Click "Continue".

3. A screen will appear asking you to confirm your account. Click Continue.

4. Enter the password for your Amazon account, and then click Finish.

5. The "Done" screen will appear. Click Finish Now (if you allow this screen to end, the home monitoring settings will not change and you will have to start over in step 1).

There are two more settings on your device that you can configure here, and we'll cover them in the next section. Even the previous generation Echo Show 8 has the setting to become a security camera.

Add video delay or audio notification to improve privacy

Before closing the settings menu completely, you should consider two more options, both related to privacy.

Turning on the first switch marked with a video delay blurs the first few seconds of the video, as does what happens to the incoming call. This gives anyone on the other side of the camera a chance to react when they are suddenly being watched. How do they know they suddenly appeared in front of the camera, you ask?

They will know if you decide to turn on another switch on this screen, the one called Sound Alerts. If this setting is on, the device plays a sound when the camera starts broadcasting, allowing all other ends to know that the camera channel is working. With home monitoring, you can check on children from a nearby Echo Show 5 without using the Alexa two-way call feature called Drop-In.

If you live alone, these settings may not be useful to you. But if you live with other people - whether family or friends - you should warn them if they are interviewed, so you can include both.

How to watch the security cameras video and audio feed

Now comes the most interesting part - test your camera. Please note: if you are doing this from the same room as the camera you entered, you will need to mute your phone or tablet to avoid sound responses. Here are the steps:

1. Open Alexa and tap Devices in the bottom menu.

2. Scroll to the top menu and tap Camera.

3. Touch the Echo Show device with the camera you want to view.

Then the program will open the camera channel. If you're using the latest version of Echo Show 10, you can swipe left or right to pan the camera and double-tap or squeeze to zoom in and out.

On the display screen:

SATURDAY, JUNE 1
Toronto, ON

22° | 20°

Try "Alexa, what's the weather in Toronto."

Pro advice. Rotate your phone or tablet to a horizontal position to get the largest and best view of your device's camera. In landscape mode, you can tap the screen with one touch to call up the speaker and microphone controls or return to the camera bar.

CHAPTER FIVE

How to Add Skills to an Echo Show

There are actually several ways to add skills to your Echo Show (or Echo Spot) - and it shouldn't be much different from how you set them up on a regular Alexa speaker.

1. Ask Alexa

The easiest way to add a skill to a shielded Echo device is to simply say, "Alexa, enable [skill name]. Or, if you want to delete a skill, simply say," Alexa, disable it. "Return [skill name]." If you're not sure what skills to add - even after reading our comprehensive list below - you can ask a few: "Alexa, recommend me some skills." You can also do this for different skill categories, such as news, smart home, and games.

2. Using Alexa App

Another way to add skills is to have Alexa on your iOS or Android device.

- Open Alexa.
- Click more.
- Click Skills and Games.
- Find the skill you want to add to your collection.
- On the skill description page, you'll see the Enable for use option - tap it.

3. Use the Amazon website

The easiest accessible method to download Alexa skills is via the Amazon website itself.

- Open Amazon in your web browser.
- Go to Shopping> Echo & Alexa> Alexa Skills.

- On the right is the Enable option - tap it.

The best Alexa app and skills

Now you can make video calls with contacts and via Echo Show or Echo Spot via "Alexa, call mom on Skype".

Amazon Prime Video

You can watch TV shows and movies from Amazon Prime Video on your Amazon Echo Show and Spot if you have the main account. To watch shows such as The Grand Tour and Bosch (surprisingly not a dishwasher show), just say "Alexa, play [show name] on Amazon Prime Video".

Calendar

Okay, not Alexa skills - but more useful than most of the skills on this list. You can connect and view the calendar on the Alexa screen. Open Alexa to connect calendars from Microsoft, Gmail, and Apple, among others.

1. Click Add.

2. Tap Settings.

3. Scroll down to Calendar and Email.

4. Select a calendar service and share your calendar and/or e-mail.

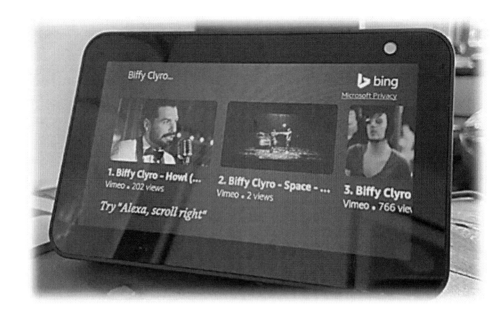

Dailymotion / Vimeo

The video on Amazon Echo broke down after a dispute between Google and Amazon, which meant that YouTube support was discontinued from Alexa devices. Fortunately, Dailymotion and Vimeo have entered a void - with a little help from Microsoft's Bing; but no official skills were found.

"Alexa, play music video Biffy Clyro" will start searching for the video you want to watch and you will get the results on the screen from the two services. Suitable for music videos and entertainment - but people with different tastes may find it desirable. This is a good break until Vevo appears.

WikiHow

Sometimes you just want to learn how to do something, and you need good textbooks for that. Enter the WikiHow skill, which will give you video tutorials on how to do almost anything. All you have to do is say something like, "Alexa, ask WikiHow how to tie my shoelaces," and you'll be in the race.

Nest

A blessing for smart home fans, you can say Alexa, show me my front door to request this security camera tape appear on the Echo Show screen - obviously. This is a replacement for the "front door" in the name of your Nest Cam. This can turn your camera into a great monitor for your child or just work as a seamless way to check what's going on in different areas of the house.

Ring

In another smart home integration function, you can ask "Alexa, show my Ring Doorbell" to report what's happening on the street. You don't even have to wait for the alarm - you can pull out the feed at any time. However, some drawbacks are that the channel is not displayed automatically on the Ring and there is no two-way sound. However, it is still useful to weed out those who waste time calling.

Good housekeeping

A skill that boils down to everything from recipes to tips on how to remove stains from upholstered furniture is like, "Alex, ask a good housekeeper what to do for dinner tonight." The screen helps recipes, making it one of the best, best home management skills.

Train Your Brain

You can fix puzzles with a variety of puzzle skills. You can try saying "Alexa, open brain training - the odd one out" for a series of visual tasks, the more difficult the task, the longer the game. Up to four players can work with it. If that's not enough, say "Alexa, turn on Quick Fire Quiz", which will lead to questions.

Stream player

Say "Alexa, run stream player" to get a bunch of indie video content from NASA, Bloomberg, and CBS. Here's what to see and do - and it's definitely a great alternative to trying to watch serious TV shows on Netflix and Amazon Prime Video.

How to pair a Bluetooth device

Amazon Alexa devices allow you to transfer audio through other speakers connected via Bluetooth.

Before you begin:

- Place the Echo and the Bluetooth speaker at least three feet away. When the Echo device is near an external speaker, Alexa may find it harder to hear wake-up words and other requests.
- For best results, use a certified Bluetooth speaker for use with Echo devices. For more information, visit the Amazon support page titled "Supported Bluetooth profiles and certified echo speakers"
- Make sure you can connect the speaker to other Bluetooth devices, such as mobile phones.
- Turn on the Bluetooth speaker and turn up the volume.

- Other Bluetooth gadgets should be disconnected from the Echo device. Echo devices can only connect to one Bluetooth device at a time.

How to watch YouTube videos

Ask Alexa to open YouTube on the Echo Show

- **"Alexa, open YouTube".**

If this is your first request, Alexa will ask you to select the default browser. Your options include Amazon's Silk or

Mozilla's Firefox. Tap the browser to select a browser (you don't have to do this again for future requests to open YouTube). Note that if you prefer Firefox to Silk, you can also use YouTube TV, as Firefox is one of the few browsers other than Chrome that supports YouTube TV.

Alexa will then open YouTube directly in the browser of your choice. Whether or not you can sign in to your YouTube account is up to you. From now on, to use YouTube on the Echo Show, ask Alexa to open YouTube, and the website will open. Tap the Echo Show touch screen to log in, or search and navigate YouTube like on a tablet. You can ask things like "Alexa, play SNL on YouTube," but Alexa will search and show a YouTube results page that you can click to play the video.

Does not work? You may need an update

If you are using an older Echo Show, make an update to the present software.

- Scroll down from the upper part of the device screen.
- Click Install.
- Go to Device Settings.

- Update your software by checking for software updates.

Then your Echo Show will be updated. This will allow you to use YouTube.

How to Use Netflix on Your Amazon Echo Show

If you don't know if Netflix is running on your device, follow the steps in the "Netflix Settings" section.

Features of Netflix

Netflix is available on the Amazon Echo Show. Netflix streaming features on supported devices include:

Navigation

Scroll down after launching the program to see the suggested genres. Click Browse to view a specific category. Click Search to find a TV show or movie. To fast forward and rewind, tap anywhere on the screen, and then slide your finger along the progress bar to rewind the title. Press the back button to exit the movie.

Resolution

The Echo Show broadcasts Netflix TV shows and movies with a resolution of up to 540p SD.

Subtitles and alternative audio

During playback, click the bubble at the top of the screen to adjust the subtitles and sound in another language.

Amazon Alexa

Control playback or play the title with voice controls using Amazon Alexa.

Configure Netflix

The Netflix application is installed automatically, and there is no need to download the Echo Show. To connect Echo Show to your Netflix account, make sure you're on the home screen and follow these steps:

Connect from the home screen

- Swipe from the home screen, and select Video.
- On the Videos tab, select the Netflix icon.
- Select Login for participants.

Set up your membership in case you are not yet a member.

- Enter your Netflix email address and password.
- Select Continue.

Your Netflix account is now linked to your device.

Connect with Alexa

- Open Netflix by saying "Alexa, open Netflix"
- Select Login for participants.

Set up your membership in case you are not yet a member.

- Enter your Netflix email address and password.
- Select Continue.

Netflix account is now connected to the gadget.

Zoom set up for Echo Show

Overview of the setup process:

- Download the Alexa mobile app.
- Connect your calendar to Alexa. (Recommendations)
- Set up an Echo Show with your Alexa account.
- Sign in to zoom in on your Echo Show. (Recommendations)

Download the Alexa mobile app

Follow the instructions here to download and install Alexa on your mobile device. After installation, log in or create a new account.

Connect your calendar to Alexa

To easily join appointments, we recommend that you connect your calendar to Alexa. This will allow you to ask Alexa to start your zoom appointment by saying "Alexa start my zoom appointment". Find the calendar you want to use for zoom meetings. To connect a calendar to Alexa, follow these steps:

- Open Alexa.
- Tap the advanced options icon and tap Settings
- Tap Calendar and email.
- Select the provider of your account, then click Connect Account.
- Follow the on-screen instructions to link the calendar. For each calendar, you want to connect, repeat these procedures.

Note. When your calendar account is linked, your calendar copy is stored in the cloud so by using Alexa you can access it. Content from your calendar can be accessed by anyone who uses your Alexa device.

By default, Alexa also includes any calendars you subscribe to in Google Calendar. Be sure to turn off calendars that you do not want to use to join the meeting.

Set up an Echo Show with your Alexa account

After unpacking the Echo Show and connecting the supplied power adapter, follow the on-screen instructions to complete the Echo Show setup.

Sign in to zoom in on your Echo Show

If you have a Zoom account, you should sign in to Zoom for Home to get the best experience. To log in, just say "Alexa, open Zoom" and follow the instructions to set up Zoom for Home here.

Use the zoom on the Echo Show

You can join Echo Show meetings in three ways:

- Providing a meeting ID
- From your Alexa-related calendar
- From the calendar associated with your Zoom account

Join the meeting without logging in:

You can ask Alexa to join the meeting by saying "Alexa, join my meeting Zoom", and Alexa will ask you for your meeting ID and password. You can ask Alexa to join the meeting by saying "Alexa, join my meeting Zoom", and Alexa will ask you for your meeting ID and password. If, after one attempt, Alexa can't determine your ID and password for the meeting, Zoom for Home will open, and you can join the meeting manually from the touch screen. Alphanumeric meeting IDs are not supported.

Join meetings from a linked calendar via Alexa:

If your calendar is associated with Alexa, you can join future appointments by saying "Alexa, join my appointment." Alexa will analyze the merge details from your calendar and start the meeting.

Join a meeting from the calendar associated with your Zoom account:

If you are logged in to Zoom for Home on your Echo Show 8, your upcoming appointments will be displayed on the touch screen when you open Zoom by saying "Alexa, open

Zoom". You can join a future meeting by pressing the join button displayed on the touch screen.

How to Add and Upload Photos

Create a slide show on your nightstand or kitchen counter

Because Alexa's smart displays have taken over our homes, one of the best talents is a way to enjoy photos. These screens are time-consuming, doing very little, so why not use them to add a decorative style to a room during downtime? You can change the background to your own photo for great personalization and even make a slide show. The Amazon Echo Show line, which has expanded over the year to include the 5-inch Echo Show and Echo Show 8 - and the new Echo Show 10 - means there are more ways to share your memories.

There are two ways to do this on a smart Echo display that uses Amazon Photos or Facebook. We'll walk you through both below.

Add Facebook Photos to Echo Show

Your chances of having a Facebook account are much higher than your chances of using Amazon Photos, so we'll start here Of course, there's also a good chance that you have bad photos from school parties that you don't want to show when Grandma comes for tea - don't worry, you can choose which albums to share.

However, you first need to connect your Facebook account to Alexa. So, do the following:

1. Open the Alexa application on your smartphone.

2. Click More on the bottom panel

3. Select Settings.

4. Scroll down to Photos.

5. On Facebook, click Link Accounts.

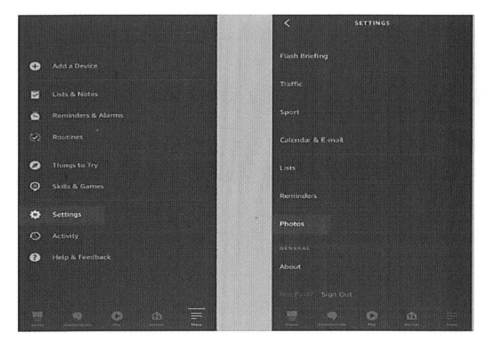

You will be redirected to a page where you need to log in to your Facebook account and give Alexa permission to access your photos. To make them appear on the Echo Show or Spot screen, do the following:

1. Swipe from the top of the screen on your Echo device, and tap Settings.

2. Click "Home and Clock."

3. Then tap Clock.

4. Click "Personal Photo."

5. Select "Background".

6. Click "Facebook".

7. Then select the album (s) you want to connect to Alexa.

8. Click "Save" at the bottom of the screen, and you're done.

Your Echo device will now display your photo on Facebook in the background. If you want to change the dial on the photo, go back to Personal Photos and select "Dial" instead. You can also ask Alexa to show your photos in a rotating carousel, saying "Alexa, show my photos" or "Alexa, show my photo albums".

Tips for improving the quality of video calls

For many of us, video calling is an important part of both our work and our personal lives, but many still forget to take a few simple steps to get the best experience. From improving lighting settings to improving sound, here are a few simple steps to make sure you get the most out of setting up video calls - no matter what you use. Use any software or hardware.

Optimize your Internet

Ethernet cable.

If you use a desktop or laptop computer for video chat, one way to reduce call problems is to make sure you have the strongest Internet connection. You can do this by switching from Wi-Fi to a wired connection by connecting an Ethernet Internet cable directly to your computer.

However, keep in mind that camera lenses perfectly remove stains and smudges that can damage the image of others in your conversation. To avoid these risks, gently wipe the lens with a soft cloth before making a video call.

Create enough light

Whether you're chatting with friends or discussing with a colleague, setting the right lighting is one of the easiest ways to look your best during a video call. First, make sure that the main light source - natural or artificial - is not directly behind you, as this will turn your head into a silhouette. In other words, make sure the main light is on your face to emphasize your features.

If there is no natural light in your room, experiment with ceiling lights and any lights you have. If these artificial lights seem too hard, try placing a little parchment around the light source to scatter it. Nowadays, you can find a wide selection of USB lights designed specifically for video calling, so it's relatively easy to find the perfect light for your workspace, no matter where it is.

Get the right angle

The camera angle is also important for high-quality images. If it rises too high or down too low, the camera may distort your functions and make you look weird. To avoid this, try to make sure the camera is at eye level so that it can best and most accurately depict what you actually look like.

If you're calling from a smartphone, you'll probably want to keep your phone in landscape mode, especially if you know that most people involved in a call use a PC. Also, try to hold the handheld device firmly or place it on something stable, otherwise, the image will constantly shake, leaving others wondering if an earthquake has occurred.

Set up the microphone

If you use a desktop or laptop computer, do you know where the microphone is? Make sure nothing is blocking or obscuring so that the people involved in your conversation can hear you without having to constantly squat or fiddle with the volume buttons.

You should also consider the acoustics of the room in which you are. If your voice is heard a little, it will sound much worse for everyone else involved in the call. Covering hard surfaces with a sheet or blanket can help reduce sound and eliminate echoes. You can also improve the sound quality of calls by using an external USB microphone or similar device.

Take a pair of earbuds

Your device's built-in speakers should work fine in most cases, but to be safe, consider using paired headphones to get the best chance of catching everything. Video chat. Using a headset also ensures that other people in the virtual room do not experience echoes or other feedback that causes the microphone to hear the speaker sound, which can be annoying and annoying. Some video calling platforms use echo cancellation, but this is not always reliable.

How to Drop In

With Amazon Echo, you can use other Echo devices, allowing you to communicate with friends and family through a smart speaker. Although you cannot access people without permission, you can log in on Echo devices at home and on contacts that Alexa has permitted you to. You can even start group chats by dropping "anywhere" (on all Echo devices in your household). This feature is an interesting way to keep abreast of what's going on in your home.

Step 1: Download app

First, make sure you've downloaded Alexa to your Android or iOS device (and this is the latest version). You'll need two different Echo devices to run Drop In: you can sign in to other Echo devices with the app, but you can't receive Drop In calls through the app. After downloading and running the program, you will be prompted to set up the call and text on Alexa. If not, tap the tooltip at the bottom of the screen to register and enter your contact information.

Step 2: Activate Drop-in on devices

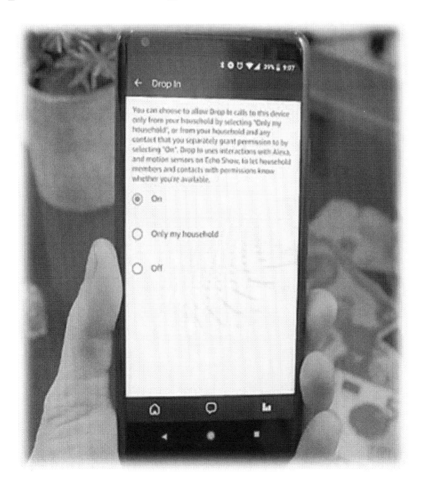

The Drop In feature can be disabled in the app, so you may have to choose to use Drop In. Go to the icon at the bottom of Alexa that says Devices. In the device menu, select the device for which you want to enable the Drop In feature. In the Echo device settings, find the "Media" section and select it. The "Communications" section will have a "Login" section. Make sure Drop In is turned on. You can select it and choose between On, Off and My Home Only.

If you enable Drop In on all of your Echo devices, you can initiate home sign-in sessions by simply saying, "Alexa, sign in," and then saying your specific name. Echo device. If that's all you want to do, then you should go. However, you can also enable sign-in outside of your home if you wish, and permitted contacts will be able to log in to your Echo.

Step 3: Enable profile Drop In

To make Drop In calls through Alexa and get others to do the same, you need to enable Drop In in your profile. Fortunately, this is very easy to do. Just select the tooltip at the bottom of Alexa, then select the Drop In icon at the top. Alexa will appear with a message on how to enable Drop In by going to My Profile. Once there, make sure the Enable section is enabled, and if it wasn't already, select it to enable it.

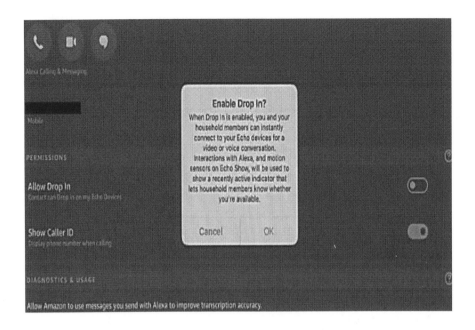

Step 4: Enable contact Drop In and ask them to do similar thing

Now it's time to enable Drop In for your other contacts. Select the Connect icon again, select the person icon in the upper right corner to go to your contacts, and select the contact you want to chat with. You will notice that they have Alexa Call & Text under their name if they have an Echo device or an Alexa account, prompting you to enable Drop In for them. In the "Permissions" section, make sure that the "Allow Drop In" option is selected for the contacts for which you want to enable Drop In on your device.

Step 5: Start calling

Once set up, you are ready to call. You activate a feature by saying the word you chose to activate its abilities, then say "Drop In [person's name]" and your device rings that person. You can also go directly to the contacts page and choose who you want to call.

When someone Drop In on you, the light ring on your Echo will start pulsing green, an alarm will sound, and they will be connected automatically, allowing them to hear everything within range of the device. If you and your contact use devices with a screen, the video will look a bit distorted for a few seconds, so you have a chance to be ready. There are verbal and tactile options for exiting the video during a call, such as saying "turn off video" or pressing the on-screen button to turn off the video.

How to manually add contacts to your Alexa device

Open Alexa on your mobile phone, tap "Communication" in the bottom menu. Tap the humanoid icon in the upper right corner. Tap the 3 dots in the upper right corner to the right of the word Contacts. Click "Add contact" and enter your contact information. Click here for more information on adding and editing contacts. Now that you've added a contact to your list, learn more about setting up Alexa Check-in and how to get reminders to keep in touch with friends and family with Alexa Connections.

CHAPTER SIX-Tips and Tricks

Stop (or start) the background

To change the background image on your Echo Show, open Alexa, tap the hamburger menu at the bottom right and go to Settings> Device Settings. Find your Echo Show and tap Photo Display. Here you can link your Echo Show with photos on your phone, Amazon Photos, or Facebook account. You can also include "Daily Memories" or "This Day" for highlights; select only a few photos manually, or just select a photo. Say "Alexa, go to settings" (or swipe down and tap Settings), then tap Home screen and clock> Clocks & photos> Profile photo> Backgrounds, and select the service related to the services you want to use.

Prepare silk installation

Silk is a browser that Amazon offers on most Fire devices. (Amazon used to offer Firefox as an option, but the deal fell through in April.) So if you're browsing any websites, make sure Silk is set up to place your bets. Go to Settings> Device settings> Web settings> Browser> Browser settings. Silk can scale web pages, store passwords, provide secure browsing from unsafe sites, and clear browsing data such as history and cookies. In the Advanced section, you can also change the search engine used from Bing to Google, Yahoo, or DuckDuckGo.

Watch YouTube via Silk

The Echo Show does not have its own YouTube app, but you can watch videos on YouTube by going to the Silk browser ("Alexa, open Silk") and downloading m.youtube.com (mobile site).) Tap the bookmark icon on the toolbar above, to make it a bookmark.

View streaming services

Previously, it was the only own video player on the Echo Show, of course, Amazon Prime Video. There is now support for more (at least for now). For example, say "Alexa, start Netflix" to display the program. I couldn't get Hulu to work, but I found YouTube (via a browser), Food Network Kitchen, RedBull TV, and Tubi.

Sound Equalizer

Like any good speaker, the Echo Show has an equalizer that allows you to adjust the bass, midrange, and treble levels. You can find it by going to Settings> Sound> Equalizer on the Echo Show. Or go to Devices> [Your echo program]> [gear icon]> Sound settings. Then drag the sliders where you want them. But you don't really need to access the sliders. Just say "Alexa, tun up the treble" or "Alexa, lower bass" and so on. And if that sounds awful, shout "Alexa, reset the equalizer." (Equalizers are also available for Echo devices without a screen, only with voice commands or a mobile application.)

Play Karaoke night with stars

Do you have Amazon Music? You do this if you have Amazon Prime, which means you get access to about 2 million songs to play on your Echo Show. (Pay extra for Amazon Music Unlimited for over 70 million ringtones.) What's really great is that most of these songs have lyrics that you can watch in real-time when the music is playing, line by line, right on the Echo screen Show. Tap the screen and you'll get controls to pause, skip back and forth in an album or playlist, set the playlist to random, or repeat the list. (Unfortunately, lyrics are not displayed on competing music streaming services, such as Pandora or Spotify.)

Set the brightness

Scroll down from the upper part of the Echo screen for fast access to Settings and Do Not Disturb (DND) (or you can say Alexa, Do Not Disturb). Using it darkens everything for a while and it won't light up when you move in front of it. More importantly, there is a slider to set the screen brightness from 1 to 10. This is the only way to do it. If you say "Alexa, set the brightness to 10", it will simply tell you to swipe down the screen.

Set Do not disturb

You can enable Do Not Disturb (DND) by swiping down or saying Alexa, enable do not disturb, or Alexa, do not disturb me. DND prevents Alexa from bothering you and prevents you from receiving video calls from people you know who also have Alexa-based devices. The smart thing is to plan it periodically until DND. In the Alexa mobile app, go to Settings> Device Settings and find your Echo Show. Select the gear icon in the upper right corner, then select Do Not Disturb> Scheduled. Set the start and end times. This will prevent subscribers from visiting you via Alexa during your break and will darken the screen during this time.

Turn off the screen

Want a short break from the light of the tiny Echo Show screen? You do not need to turn off the power completely. Say, "Alexa, turn off the screen," and she'll be gone. By muttering the wake word or tapping the screen again, will turn it on. (Just using the on-screen slide dimmer isn't a completely blank screen.)

Get on trailer

Almost every movie trailer you can think about is available to view on the Echo Show, and all you just need to do is say, Alexa, show me the movie trailer [TITLE]. Sometimes it is quite demanding on the name; Saw: Spiral does not work, but Spiral: Saw works.

Restrict access to search and videos

Do you have a child or two at home using the Echo Show to view or search for questionable material? Block them. On the Echo Show, go to Settings> Restrict Access. From there, you can restrict access to the following:

- Amazon Photos (Note. This will prevent photos as a slideshow background.)
- Trailer
- Web browser (blocks all searches)
- Web Video Search (You can enable SafeSearch to restrict adult content.)
- Video provider

Note that some of the above changes may require you to enter your Amazon password and two-factor authentication code if enabled. You can use the Alexa mobile app on your smartphone to activate Amazon Kids (formerly known as FreeTime) to enable parental controls, which goes even further by setting time limits and even pausing the device with small buttons.

It is likely that you do not really want to talk to your Alexa device. On the Echo Show with display, you can set "Tap to Alexa" - the icon that touches the finger that remains on the screen (you can move it). Tap and you'll see a screen with options for quickly entering questions, checking the weather, setting a timer, receiving news, setting alarms, checking your shopping list, and more - you're controlling what's on the screen. This is great for checking out the Echo Show in the dark when it can interfere with someone talking - or if you're using the show as an alarm clock by the bed.

To set the Click Alexa button, go to Settings> Accessibility> Tap Alexa. To control the Alexa touch screen, tap and click the Control button. If you click "Add New", you can enter what you normally ask Alexa to do - for example, start the "Echo Show" skill, and set it as a button so you don't have to repeat it.

Call and text without Speech

Like clicking on Alexa, "Speechless Communication" displays the decryption of messages left by your contacts or family members on your Alexa device, and allows you to send them messages by tapping on the Echo Show screen. Turn it on in Settings> Accessibility> Communication without speech.

You can also access your contacts on the screen using the vertical three-point menu that appears on the home screen. If you don't like typing - which can be confusing on the Echo Show - there's a microphone icon on the front and center so you can say something that needs to be rewritten. Naughty words are moderated using the Echo Show program on the screen (but you can always view interrupted original messages in the Alexa mobile app on your phone).

Take a selfie

It's easy. Make a statement such as Alexa, take a selfie, and after a warning and a countdown of 3, the Echo Show's front camera will snap a photo of you, including a preview on the screen, and then saves it to Amazon Photos.

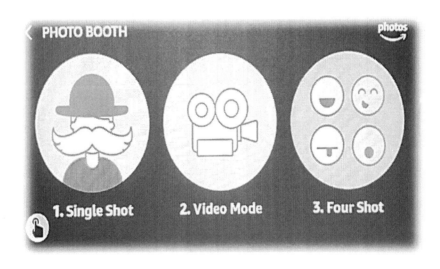

However, there are more options than this. You can say "Alexa, share this photo" to include the photo in the album in Amazon Photos. Or wait and this will open Photo Booth so you can take another shot, a short video or 4 shots like you were at the kiosk at the festival. Then check out the Photo Booth album, which shows all the pictures taken with the Echo Show in Amazon Photos.

Barcode scanner

The Echo Show front camera will not only take your photos but also scan barcodes for products. Say "Alexa, scan" and place the barcode in the barcode on the screen. If the product is in the Amazon catalog, it will be added to your shopping list.

DONE

**Hacks For Alexa
has been added to your shopping list**

Try "Alexa, show my shopping list"

Allow Echo Show to read screen

One of the features of the Echo Show is VoiceView Screen Reader - it makes the program read aloud everything that appears on the screen. You can turn it on in a variety of ways, but the easiest way is to say "Alexa, turn VoiceView on or off. To configure settings, go to Settings> Availability> VoiceView Screen Reader." include setting the reading speed, the default volume for the voice compared to the sound, how much will be displayed, the program is performed by various gestures with several fingers.

Reading Magnification

Go to Settings> Accessibility> Magnifier and turn it on. You can then tap the screen three times to enlarge what you see. You can then squeeze or release with two fingers to zoom in or out.

Identify something with Show and tell

Amazon identifies goods well - it's better to sell something to you. If you or someone you know has poor eyesight and you can't tell what canned food they can open, Echo Show can help with Show and Tell. Say "Alexa what am I holding" and hold the item in front of the camera a foot away. Echo shows can help you line up or rotate goods properly. Then, if he can say what kind of product it is, he will say it out loud for you.

CHAPTER SEVEN

Podcast Listener

Listen without skills.

By default, Alexa serves podcasts via TuneIn. If you ask, "Alex, play Revisionist history podcast," it will trigger the last episode of the service. Although you can't name a specific podcast episode, you can play the episode before the currently playing episode: "Alexa, play the previous episode." If you temporarily switch to an alternative source for podcasts, music, or audio, Alexa may not be able to resume where you left off; You will need to start from scratch.

You can also ask Alexa to simply "play the podcast" and it will play a podcast that you definitely don't like. (The niche nature of podcasts is what makes them great. Look for podcasts that match your unique interests.)

Play podcasts with Alexa.

You can also use Alexa to search and manage podcasts.

- Open Alexa on your mobile device or at alexa.amazon.com.

- From the main menu, select Music, Videos, and Books.

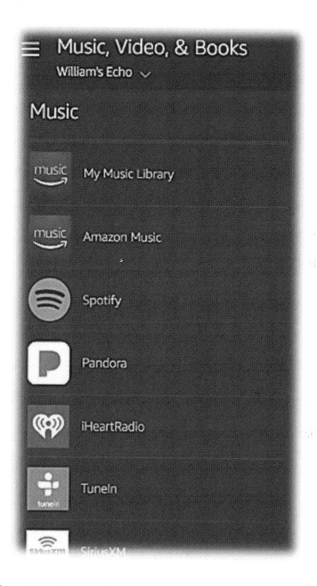

- In the Music section, select TuneIn.

Select Podcasts.

- You can also use the TuneIn search bar at any time to find a specific podcast.

- Explore categories to find an interesting podcast and then a specific episode.

- At the upper part of the app, select the desired speakers.

- Click on the podcast cover to play.

Listen to podcast with AnyPod.

Among them, AnyPod is still the most popular. It also offers the highest level of reliability, which, unfortunately, says very little about its quality. In addition to Alexa's limited capabilities by default, AnyPod can play certain episodes, go to a specific time, and even manage subscriptions. However, the service does not have an application - mobile, web, or other - or any intuitive interface, which makes it difficult for listeners to juggle multiple podcasts. Some AnyPod commands include:

Alexa, request AnyYod to play the episode [number] [Podcast name].

Alexa, request AnyPod [fast forward / rewind] [duration].

Alexa, play [next / previous] series.

Alexa, request AnyPod about the [latest / oldest] episode.

Alexa request AnyPod to register [Podcast Name].

Alexa, request AnyYod to unsubscribe from [Podcast Name].

Alexa, request AnyPod: "What is my subscription?"

Alexa, request AnyYod to play my podcast.

Enable podcast skills

Like all Alexa skills, you can enable AnyPod and Alexa in the Alexa application or with voice commands.

Activate skills through the Alexa app.

Open Alexa on your mobile device or at alexa.amazon.com.

- From the main menu, select Skills.
- Look for AnyPod or Stitcher.

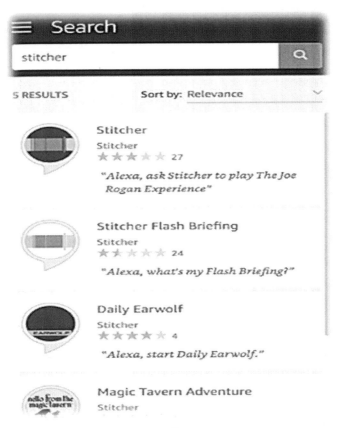

- In the results, select the desired skill.
- Click Enable Skills.

Activate your skills with voice commands.

Just ask, "Alexa, enable [AnyPod / Stitcher]."

Stream via your favorite podcast app

If you're interacting with Alexa through a smart headset or Bluetooth-enabled speaker, you can connect that device to your phone or tablet and then play podcasts from your favorite app. While Alexa control will be limited to basic features such as playback, pause, and volume control, it will give you the best control over managing your subscriptions. To connect your Echo to your phone or tablet, follow these steps:

- Make sure your device is within range of the Echo speaker.
- Disconnect all existing Bluetooth connections using the "Alexa, disconnect" command.
- Put your smartphone, tablet or other device in Bluetooth mode.

- Switch the Echo device to pairing mode with the "Alexa, pair" command. She will confirm: "I'm looking for ..."

- On your phone, tablet, or other devices, select the Echo speaker in the Bluetooth settings. Alexa will let you know that the connection was successful.

- After setting up the connection, you can restart it at any time when devices within range, with Bluetooth, are active by executing the command "Alexa, pair with [Device Name]" or "Alexa, connect to [Device Name]".

Connect Spotify with Alexa

- Download and open Alexa.
- Tap the menu in the upper left corner.
- Tap Settings, then tap Music and podcasts.
- Select Spotify, then link your account to Alexa.
- Log in to your Spotify account.

Make Spotify default

Set it so you don't have to say "on Spotify" at the end of voice commands:

- In Alexa, tap the menu in the upper left corner.

- Tap Settings, then tap Music and podcasts.

- Click Select default music service.

- Select Spotify and tap DONE.

Note: You still need to say "on Spotify" at the end of the podcast commands.

Now just ask Alexa to play something like "Alexa, play Discover Weekly".

CHAPTER EIGHT

Book restaurant with Alexa

You don't have to go through complicated audio menus or flip through confusing websites to provide a table for a night out. With OpenTable Skills with Alexa you can book restaurants right from your Echo show. All you have to do is say, "Alexa, ask OpenTable to reserve a table for me" or "Alexa, ask OpenTable to make a reservation". Enter the name of the restaurant, as well as the date and time of booking, and you will rush - or maybe just go out to dinner.

Monitor your baby with Echo show

Let's say you're a new parent with lots of security cameras, but you don't have the money to buy a special monitor for children. After all, diapers are unreasonably expensive. Alexa can act as a baby monitor - just install an Alexa-compatible security camera in your child's nursery, like the Logitech Circle 2, and then you'll be able to watch the live broadcast on your Echo Show.

Amazon Echo Show Baby Review

Alexa works with many brands of security cameras, including Ring, Nest, Logitech, Netgear, and a lot of others. Just ask Alexa to show the tape from your security camera on your Echo Show and you can watch your kids as they doze off.

Enable celebrity sound for Alexa

If you're tired of the same whimsical voice on your same weird smart speaker, the good news is: Alexa may sound like a celebrity. You can change Alex's voice to sound like

103

Samuel L. Jackson. Although the voice only works for certain commands, there is a certain amount of fun in polling your smart display and getting an answer from the king of attitudes. You can even say "Hey, Samuel" to activate the assistant, instead of the much more common "Hey Alex".

And if you have young children at home, there is even better news: you can turn off Jackson's signature pot on your Alexa. The B089NGHR7K costs $ 3, but it's worth it.

Traffic Check

If you're like most people, you have at least two different ways to get started - the "quick" way to the direct path and the "best" way to avoid backing up your traffic. The last thing you want is to walk out the door without knowing what kind of traffic is expected.

All you have to do is ask, "Alex, how's the traffic jam?" Of course, you will need to set the start and end points in the Settings menu. Alexa will offer the fastest route to work if traffic is supported on your regular route.

Communicate with others voiceless

We usually perceive our smart assistants as fully voice technology, but this is not always the case. Echo Show has a virtual keyboard that can be activated via the Accessibility menu. Swipe down from the top of the screen and tap Settings> Availability and scroll down until Touch appears. Move the slide to the on position, and then click Continue.

A small icon appears in the lower-left corner of the screen. Tap it to open a new menu, then tap the quick questions icon to open the virtual keyboard. You can send commands to your smart home, ask Alexa to complete tasks, and more. You can also do this directly from the Alexa app on your smartphone.

CHAPTER NINE-Troubleshooting

These are some of the reasons why Alexa and your Echo device may not work properly together. There may be a simple culprit, such as a power outage or the Internet. Echo devices may be grouped incorrectly, or there may be problems with Wi-Fi. You may have a problem with voice recognition or a problem with setting up your Amazon account. Regardless of the cause of your error in Alexa and Echo communication, some simple troubleshooting steps will help you sync them quickly.

Lots of these troubleshooting techniques overlap from one problem to another. This is because a potential problem with Alexa devices and Alexa-enabled devices can cause some problems.

Here are the 8 most common Alexa and Echo issues that users face with Alexa and their Echo devices, as well as some simple fixes.

Full reset

An echo show that creates problems? First, follow the entire "disconnect and connect" procedure. You can also turn off the echo show by holding down the mute button for a few seconds. (Turn it on again by holding down the mute button again.) If that doesn't work, delete it, so to speak, by resetting it to factory settings and starting anew. Say "Alexa, go to settings" and tap Device settings> Reset to factory defaults. This will delete all the settings you have set, from the name of your Echo Show to any associated accounts. You will have to go through the setup process again.

You can use the Alexa mobile app to activate this too. Go to Settings> Device Settings> find your Echo Show and tap the gear icon> Reset to factory settings.

Fix Alexa not responding to voice commands

Sometimes you give voice commands, but your Alexa and Echo don't respond and don't respond to things like "Sorry, I don't know this command" or "Sorry, I don't understand you now. Please try again later..." Alexa is not responding properly, there are a few simple fixes you can try.

Be sure that your Echo has power access and proper internet coverage. This is a simple, basic troubleshooting step, but it's worth making sure. Echoes of not connecting or disconnecting from the Internet can be the reason that Alexa ignores you.

Make sure the Echo microphone is on. The microphone is muted if you have a solid red ring or line instead of solid blue. Press the microphone button on the top of the device to turn it on again. See if Alexa can respond to your commands.

Tip: Another low-tech trick is to move the Echo closer to where you're talking. Alex may not hear you.

Be sure your smartphone and Echo are using the same Wi-Fi coverage. If your smartphone and Alexa are on a Wi-Fi network other than your Echo, your Echo will not be able to respond. Make sure both the app and the device are on the same Wi-Fi network and then see if Alexa can hear you.

Make sure your Alexa-enabled device is within range of Wi-Fi. Alexa may not respond because your Echo is too far from the router. Move it closer to the router and see if that solves the problem.

Restart your Alexa-enabled device. A simple reboot often solves a bunch of mysterious technical problems. See if restarting your Echo solves an unresponsive Alexa problem.

Check your Wi-Fi connection. If you have problems with your Wi-Fi, reset it and see if Alexa responds.

Make sure Alexa heard your statement. If you don't speak clearly, Alexa can confuse your voice commands. Looking at Alexa's story, you may find that she thinks you said "Play Mushroom" instead of "Play Music."

Change the wake word. If your Alexa and Echo don't respond, try changing the wake-up word and see if your smart speaker and digital assistant work again.

Reset Alexa-enabled devices to factory defaults. If all else fails, try resetting your Alexa-enabled device to factory defaults to resolve the issue.

If you select this option, you will need to register the device in your Amazon account and re-enter the device settings in Alexa.

How to Fix Alexa Music Play on Wrong Device

Multi-room sound allows you to control music playback on Echo speakers. If you ask Alexa to play music on an Echo device in one room, but another Alexa-enabled device starts playing music somewhere else, there are a few solutions to try.

Make sure you create a group of smart home devices. When you add all of your smart home devices with Alexa support to your group, Alexa can respond more intelligently to your requests. For example, if you are in the kitchen and asking for music, the kitchen Echo will answer.

Tip: If the group has already been created, try deleting it and creating a new one.

Make sure the appropriate Echo is set as the selected speaker. If you want to set one of the Echos as the default speaker, specify this in the Alexa settings. Therefore, each time you request music, only the specified Echo will respond.

Name your devices Echo correctly. Echo speakers are easier to track if they are named correctly. For example, if Echo in your kitchen is named after a location, you can say, "Alexa, play Coldplay in the kitchen."

Alexa not streaming music

If Alexa doesn't seem to be able to stream music from Spotify or another streaming service, it's usually a bandwidth issue or a Wi-Fi connection. Here's what you need to do:

Check your Wi-Fi connection. If your Wi-Fi has a problem, reset it and see if it can play your music.

Reduce Wi-Fi congestion. Turn off all connected Wi-Fi devices you don't use and see if it solves your streaming issues.

Make sure your Echo is within Wi-Fi. Your Alexa-enabled device may not work properly due to its location. Move the device closer to the router and away from walls, metal objects, or other sources of interference.

Restart Echo. You should always try restarting your Alexa-enabled device. See if this solves your streaming problem.

Restart the modem and router. A simple reboot can solve any problems that occur in your modem and router. Restart the modem and router and see if it returns to streaming music.

Connect to the 5 GHz router channel. This can help minimize Wi-Fi interruptions in the 2.4 GHz band. After switching channels, try listening to the music again.

Alexa not linking to Wi-Fi

If your device has a screen, check the lighting on the device. If it appears orange, the Wi-Fi network is not properly working. Here are some ways to troubleshoot Alexa's Wi-Fi connection:

Check your internet connection. If Alexa can't connect to Wi-Fi, it may be due to a disconnected Internet connection. Check if your Internet works or not. If not, take steps to reconnect to the Internet.

Restart the modem and router. Make sure restarting the modem and router fixes Alexa's Wi-Fi connection issues.

Restart the Echo device. A simple reboot can solve problems with Alexa and Echo Wi-Fi connectivity.

Make sure your Wi-Fi password is correct. If you connect to Alexa with the wrong Wi-Fi password, this may be the cause of the problem. Check the Wi-Fi password on the other device and, if necessary, change it and try connecting Alexa again.

Make sure your Alexa-enabled device is within range of Wi-Fi. Your Alexa-enabled device may not be in the Wi-Fi range. Move the device closer to the router and away from walls, metal objects, or other sources of interference.

Reduce Wi-Fi congestion. Turn off all connected Wi-Fi devices that you are not using and see if this solves the Wi-Fi connection problem.

Reset Echo to factory settings. When all else fails and your Alexa app still doesn't connect to Wi-Fi, reset Echo to factory settings and see if it helps reconnect.

If you select this option, you will need to register the device in your Amazon account and re-enter the device settings in Alexa.

Alexa Calls not Working

The Amazon Echo can replace a home phone. If the Alexa call doesn't work, try a few troubleshooting steps.

Make sure your contact information is correct. Alexa can only call when your contacts are set up correctly. Make sure you call the booking contact who can receive calls through your Alexa device.

Check your Echo's Internet connection. Alexa cannot call if Echo is not properly connected to the

Internet. If necessary, reconnect to the Internet, and then try calling again.

Restart Alexa on your phone. A simple software failure can be a problem. Restart Alexa through the Settings menu, and then restart the program. See if this solves your call problem.

Update Alexa on your iPhone or Android. If restarting and restarting the program does not work, you may need to update the program. Go to the iTunes App Store or Google Play and see if an updated version is available. After updating the program, check if it solves the problem with the call.

Make Alexa can hear what you are saying. If you do not speak clearly, Alexa may not understand the name of the contact you are trying to call. Check your Alexa voice history. She may have heard "Call your chin" instead of "Call Gretchen."

If Alexa cannot find a device

You may be trying to add a new smart home device, but Alexa can't find it. Here's what to do:

Be sure your smart home gadget is Alexa compatible. Alexa can only detect smart devices that support Alexa.

Complete the device setup online. Go to the Amazon Amazon page and try to complete the setup there. Make sure Alexa can recognize your smart home device.

Restart Alexa on your phone. Restart Alexa through the Settings menu, and then restart the program. Make sure Alexa is able to detect your smart home gadget.

Restart the Echo device. After restarting Alexa, restart Echo, and then see if Alexa can detect it.

Be sure your smartphone and Echo are connected to the same Wi-Fi network. If your smartphone and Alexa are on different Wi-Fi networks, your Alexa will not be able to detect your Echo or other Alexa-enabled device.

Update your router settings. After updating your router settings, try asking Alexa to reopen your smart home device by saying, "Open my device."

Bluetooth connection problem

If Alexa is having trouble connecting to Bluetooth, here's what you should do:

Make sure Alexa and the Bluetooth device are connected properly. If your Echo device cannot connect to Bluetooth or the Bluetooth connection stops checking, check that you have established the connection correctly.

Update the software version on your Echo. Although your Echo will automatically receive updates, an outdated version of the software may cause problems with Bluetooth connectivity. Check the software version of your Echo device and update it if necessary.

Make sure your Bluetooth device uses a supported Bluetooth profile. Alexa now supports an advanced audio distribution profile (A2DP SNK) and a remote audio / video profile.

Disconnect and reconnect your Alexa device and Bluetooth device. Sometimes resolving a problem is solved by removing the paired Bluetooth device from Alexa and then re-pairing it.

Make sure the Bluetooth device is fully charged and close to the Echo device when you connect the two devices.

If Alexa is nor operating a certain skill

Alexa's skills are similar to voice control programs in a digital assistant. If you find that a skill like Spotify or Pandora doesn't work, here's what to do:

Check the Wi-Fi connection on your device. Alexa will not be able to perform the skill if Wi-Fi is turned off or incorrectly connected.

Make sure the skill is activated. If you or another user accidentally disables the skill, it will not work. If necessary, reactivate the skill and see if it solves the problem.

Disable and enable skills. This simple troubleshooting step sometimes causes the skill to work again.

Make sure you name the skill correctly. You need to address the correct title starting skill. For example, you can't run a Jeopardy skill by calling it a "word game." Find the exact name of the skill, and then try again.

Printed in Great Britain
by Amazon